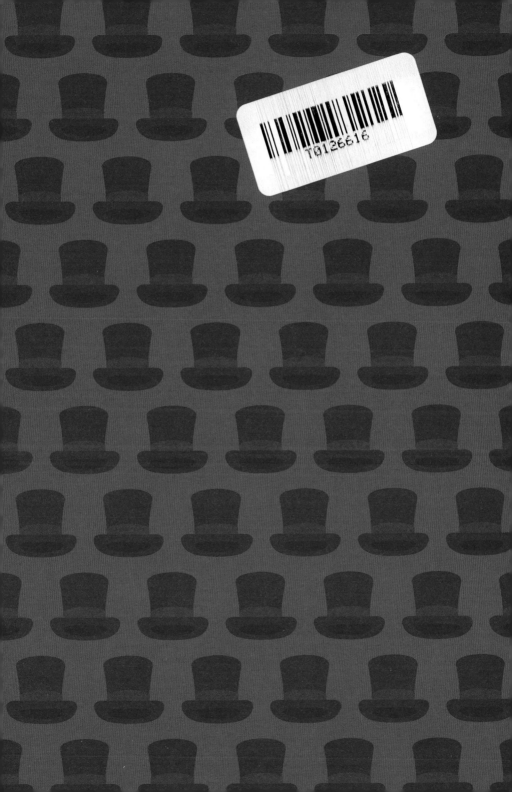

BIOGRAPHIC
DICKENS

BIOGRAPHIC
DICKENS

MICHAEL ROBB

AMMONITE
PRESS

First published 2019 by
Ammonite Press
an imprint of Guild of Master Craftsman Publications Ltd
Castle Place, 166 High Street, Lewes, East Sussex, BN7 1XU,
United Kingdom
www.ammonitepress.com

ISBN 978 1 78145 364 3

A catalogue record for this book is available from the
British Library.

Publisher: Jason Hook
Concept Design: Matt Carr
Design & Illustration: Matt Carr & Robin Shields
Editor: Jamie Pumfrey

Colour reproduction by GMC Reprographics
Printed and bound in Turkey

CONTENTS

ICONOGRAPHIC

WHEN WE CAN RECOGNIZE A WRITER BY A SET OF ICONS, WE CAN ALSO RECOGNIZE HOW COMPLETELY THAT WRITER AND THEIR WORK HAVE ENTERED OUR CULTURE AND OUR CONSCIOUSNESS.

INTRODUCTION

Charles Dickens stands alongside the likes of William Shakespeare as one of the titans of English literature. His output was prodigious – he wrote 15 large novels and numerous short stories, as well as assorted essays and journalism (amounting to over 4 million words), at the same time as editing magazines such as *Household Words* and *All the Year Round*. He is still widely read and studied around the world, and his characters remain very much alive in the public consciousness.

From poor beginnings – his father was imprisoned for debt, and Dickens himself worked in a blacking factory at the age of 12 – he rose to be an immensely popular public figure and one of the most famous writers of the 19th century. When he died in 1870, he was mourned across the entire English-speaking world.

"THERE ARE BOOKS OF WHICH THE BACKS AND COVERS ARE BY FAR THE BEST PARTS."

—Charles Dickens, *Oliver Twist*, 1837–39

His life and work are closely intertwined with the Victorian age and echo a time of great change. He is also forever linked to London, the biggest city in the world at that time, which was his home for most of his life and the backdrop to his work. He spent hours each day walking the streets of London, mulling over his latest work in progress but also gaining inspiration from the characters and events around him. He closely observed all classes of London life, and the treatment of the poor was the inspiration for many of his books, including the story of the orphan, Oliver Twist.

Dickens, unlike some authors who only achieved greatness after their death, was hugely successful as a writer while he was alive. In an era before mass media, the public got their entertainment mainly from theatrical plays and variety shows as well as magazines, newspapers and novels. Dickens' stories tapped into this demand – their appeal to the masses greatly increased by being published in monthly parts. Thousands looked forward eagerly to the next instalment of his latest novel, all of which were originally published in serial form. He led the way in raising the perception of serialized fiction as a respectable art and many other novelists (including William Makepeace Thackeray, George Eliot and Thomas Hardy) followed suit.

Dickens was a great, but flawed, family man. He married Catherine Hogarth in 1836 and together they had 10 children. Dickens loved to play games with his children, was a great story-teller and involved them in family theatricals. However, Dickens was not always faithful to Catherine. He held a strong passion for Catherine's younger sister Mary and was distraught at her early death at the age of just 17. Later, after 22 years of marriage, he left Catherine because he had fallen in love with a young actress, Ellen Ternan.

Dickens' works live on – his books are still read in many languages, re-read by successive generations and continually reimagined through film and TV adaptations. They still feature frequently on school examination syllabuses. Many of his characters, from Scrooge and Oliver Twist through to Miss Havisham and Mr Micawber, are so embedded in the public consciousness that even people who have never read his books will probably be familiar with their names.

Dickens also lives on through the many Christmas traditions his stories helped to establish, particularly through that most enduring of tales, *A Christmas Carol*, which itself popularized the greeting 'Merry Christmas!'. He also bequeathed multiple words and phrases to the English language, including 'flummoxed', 'Scrooge' and 'sawbones'.

It is hard to encapsulate all of Dickens' life and numerous achievements in one book. But the use of infographics conveys his prodigious output and the iconic nature of his literature, helping to explain why, more than 200 years after his birth, he remains on the list of the top 100 bestselling authors in the UK.

"TAKE NOTHING ON ITS LOOKS; TAKE EVERYTHING ON EVIDENCE. THERE'S NO BETTER RULE."

—Mr Jaggers, from Charles Dickens' *Great Expectations*, 1860–61

CHARLES DICKENS

01
LIFE

"WHETHER I SHALL TURN OUT TO BE THE HERO OF MY OWN LIFE, OR WHETHER THAT STATION WILL BE HELD BY ANYBODY ELSE, THESE PAGES MUST SHOW."

—Charles Dickens, *David Copperfield,* 1849–50

CHARLES DICKENS

was born on 7 February 1812 in Portsmouth, Hampshire, England

HAMPSHIRE

PORTSMOUTH

Charles John Huffham Dickens was born in Landport, a relatively new suburb of Portsmouth. Then, as now, Portsmouth was home to the Royal Navy. It had long been a fortified port, due to its strategic position on the English Channel coast, facing the threat of invasion from France for centuries. The sea, sailors and seafaring were to be themes regularly represented in Dickens' novels.

Charles' father, John Dickens, was a clerk in the Navy Pay Office. This was a busy time to be working for the Navy, as Britain had been embroiled in a war against Napoleon Bonaparte, Emperor of France, since the turn of the century.

John had married Elizabeth Barrow in 1809 and their first child, Fanny, was born in 1810. Their second, Charles, followed two years later.

At first, the family lived in a terraced house in Mile End Terrace. However, during the first six years of his life, Dickens' parents moved house five times, first within the Portsmouth area, briefly to London in 1815, and then to Chatham in Kent towards the end of 1817.

UNITED KINGDOM

LONDON

Also born in Portsmouth: ▶
Isambard Kingdom Brunel
(1806–59), famous for
building many bridges,
tunnels and railways.

WASHINGTON, D.C., USA

President James Madison declares war on the United Kingdom, a consequence of British actions in the Napoleonic Wars.

LONDON, UK

Poet Lord Byron gives his first address as a member of the British House of Lords, in defence of Luddite violence against industrialisation in Nottinghamshire.

LONDON, UK

Prime Minister Spencer Perceval is assassinated on 11 May, the only British PM to be killed in office.

CARACAS, VENEZUELA

Over 15,000 people are estimated to have died in an earthquake, measuring 7.7 on the Richter scale.

ARAPILES, SPAIN

British forces led by Wellington defeat the French at the Battle of Salamanca as part of the ongoing Peninsular War.

RUSSIA

Napoleon's *Grande Armée* (numbering over 680,000 soldiers) attempt to invade Russia. Much later, Tchaikovsky's famous *1812 Overture* was written to commemorate Russia's epic defence.

THE WORLD IN 1812

Dickens was born at a time of great turmoil and change throughout the world. The end of the 18th century had seen revolutions in the USA and France, and repercussions from both were still unfolding. Having seized power from the revolutionary government in France in 1799, Napoleon was at war with many other European countries. Britain was in the midst of the Industrial Revolution, which created major changes in daily life for millions, as jobs shifted from a rural economy to the towns and cities. This would produce further developments throughout Dickens' life, with advances in transportation (such as the steam train) making distant cities and countries easier to reach. However, while urban growth created a wider range of jobs, many thousands of people still lived in poverty and in squalid conditions, and social justice would be at the heart of much of Dickens' literature.

KASSEL, GERMANY

Children's and Household Tales by Jacob and Wilhelm Grimm, better known as *Grimms' Fairy Tales*, is published, containing 86 stories.

LIFE

DICKENS' BIG FAMILY

FATHER
John
Dickens
(1785–1851)

SISTER
Frances
'Fanny'
Dickens
(1810–48)

**Charles
Dickens**
(1812–70)

**Alfred
Dickens**
(b. & d. 1814)

SISTER
Letitia
Dickens
(1816–93)

WIFE
Catherine
Hogarth
(1815–79)

SON
Charles
'Charley'
Culliford
Boz Dickens
(1837–96)

DAUGHTER
Mary
Dickens
(1838–96)

SON
Edward
Bulwer
Lytton
Dickens
(1852–1902)

DAUGHTER
Dora
Annie
Dickens
(1850–51)

One of Dickens' great comic creations – Wilkins Micawber in *David Copperfield* – was based on his father. John ran into frequent financial troubles, spending and borrowing beyond his means. From the publication of *The Pickwick Papers* onwards, Charles had frequently to bail out his parents, supporting them for the rest of their lives.

In 1836, Charles married Catherine Hogarth, daughter of George Hogarth, editor of the *Evening Chronicle*, on which Charles was employed as a reporter. Charles and Catherine had 10 children before they separated in 1858.

There is speculation that Dickens subsequently had a child with Ellen Ternan, the young actress for whom he left his wife, but this has never been conclusively proved.

MOTHER

Elizabeth Barrow
(1789–1863)

Harriet Dickens
(b. & d. 1822)

BROTHER

Frederick Dickens
(1820–68)

BROTHER

Alfred Dickens
(1822–60)

BROTHER

Augustus Dickens
(1827–66)

DAUGHTER

Kate Macready Dickens
(1839–1929)

SON

Walter Landor Dickens
(1841–63)

SON

Francis Jeffrey Dickens
(1844–86)

SON

Henry Fielding Dickens
(1849–1933)

SON

Sydney Smith Haldimand Dickens
(1847–72)

SON

Alfred D'Orsay Tennyson Dickens
(1845–1912)

GREAT EXPECTATIONS:
DICKENS' EARLY LIFE

1812

Charles Dickens is born on 7 February in Portsmouth.

1817

The family move to Chatham, Kent, where they live for the happiest five years of Charles' childhood. Around the age of eight, Dickens writes his first story, *Misnar, Sultan of India: A Tragedy*. His father shows him Gad's Hill Place, a magnificent country house that young Charles swears he will live in one day (and he does).

1822

When Dickens is 10, the family move more permanently to London – the city that would become the backdrop to many of his major works.

1830

Falls in love with Maria Beadnell, his first grand passion. Despite many ardent letters from him, his love is unrequited.

1831

Becomes a parliamentary reporter.

1833

Publishes his first story, *A Dinner at Poplar Walk*, in the *Monthly Magazine*.

1834

Becomes a reporter on the *Morning Chronicle*, meets Catherine Hogarth (daughter of the editor of the *Evening Chronicle*) and publishes more stories and sketches of life in London.

Charles Dickens was a rather sickly child, but spending a lot of time at home meant he could discover the myriad delights of the books in his father's library (including *Tom Jones*, *Robinson Crusoe*, *Don Quixote* and the *Arabian Nights*), as well as reading innumerable magazines. At a young age, he was taken up to London to see the great clown Joseph Grimaldi at Sadler's Wells and was regularly exposed to the wonders and mysteries of the theatre, reacting with eager excitement to a multitude of plays including *Macbeth*. These influences helped nurture his love of stories and fed his imagination.

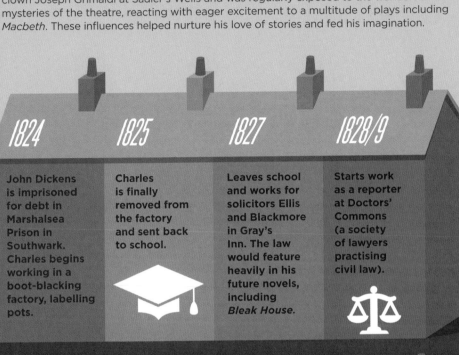

1824

John Dickens is imprisoned for debt in Marshalsea Prison in Southwark. Charles begins working in a boot-blacking factory, labelling pots.

1825

Charles is finally removed from the factory and sent back to school.

1827

Leaves school and works for solicitors Ellis and Blackmore in Gray's Inn. The law would feature heavily in his future novels, including *Bleak House*.

1828/9

Starts work as a reporter at Doctors' Commons (a society of lawyers practising civil law).

1835

Dickens and Catherine get engaged.

1836

Marries Catherine. Dickens meets John Forster, his literary advisor and future biographer. Becomes friends with the actor William Macready, the artist Daniel Maclise and the writer William Makepeace Thackeray. *Sketches by Boz*, a collection of essays on London life, is published.

1837

The Pickwick Papers is published. It is massively successful and Dickens becomes a literary sensation. His first child, Charles (known as Charley), is born. Catherine's sister Mary Hogarth dies and Dickens is distraught. He edits *Bentley's Miscellany* magazine (1837–39) and travels abroad for the first time.

LIFE

DICKENS THE DANDY

On leaving school, Dickens was keen to move away from his poor, peripatetic childhood existence and establish himself as a dapper, smart young man. In his first jobs, working for a solicitor's firm and as a parliamentary reporter, he inclined towards dandyism in his clothing and retained this style throughout his life, meticulous in always being well turned out.

Cultural society at this time was very much the preserve of the aristocracy. Dickens was seen as a bit of an *arriviste* – a brazen social climber – and his dress sense was viewed as overly colourful and rather brash, leading to him being slightly scorned by his superiors.

JEWELLERY

Dickens liked rings on his fingers and jewellery on his clothing, usually wearing a long, gold watch chain on his waistcoat.

BOOTS

Footwear was always smart and well-polished.

HAIR

A profusion of light-brown hair worn fashionably long.

FACE

A slightly feminine, handsome look to his features.

NECK TIE

A cravat or other form of neck tie, often of silk.

WAISTCOAT

Dickens was well known for his bright waistcoats in crimson or other loud colours, often patterned.

COAT

A smart coat with a high, velvet collar.

Dickens visited the USA in 1842, where the Americans, too, were suspicious of his loud dress sense.

"OUTRAGEOUSLY VULGAR – IN DRESS, MANNERS, AND MIND."

—Washington Irving

"HIS WHOLE APPEARANCE IS FOPPISH."

—*St. Louis People's Organ*

OUTSIDE

When travelling, Dickens would don a handsome blue cloak and top hat.

LIFE

DICKENS AND THE LADIES

Dickens had a complicated relationship with the women in his life. He held a romantic, idealized vision of women, which certainly led to the creation of some of his most famous female characters. From his mother to his first love Maria Beadnell, and the young actress Ellen Ternan for whom he later left his wife, Dickens was forever searching for the elusive perfect woman.

ELIZABETH DICKENS

Dickens' mother was seemingly a good-natured, easy-going woman. However, Dickens never seems to have forgiven her for sending him to a boot-blacking factory at the age of 12 to label pots.

MARIA BEADNELL

Maria was Dickens' first love, to whom he wrote countless love letters. She was the model for the beautiful but childish Dora in *David Copperfield*, whilst her rejection of Dickens (she allegedly called him a "mere boy") could also have led to the creation of the cold Estella in *Great Expectations*.

AUGUSTA DE LA RUE

Dickens befriended Augusta and her husband and, with the aid of mesmerism (which he had learned to practise), he helped relieve Augusta's severe nervous illness.

ANGELA BURDETT-COUTTS

A rich heiress and philanthropist, Angela co-founded a home for fallen women with Dickens.

CATHERINE HOGARTH

Catherine, whom he used to call his "dear Mouse" or "darling Pig", married Dickens and bore him 10 children, but he left her after 22 years of marriage.

GEORGINA HOGARTH

Catherine's younger sister Georgina joined the Dickens household at the age of 15. When Dickens left Catherine, Georgina stayed with Dickens, continuing as his housekeeper. There has been continued unconfirmed speculation about their relationship. She lived until 1917 and edited three volumes of Dickens' letters.

MARY HOGARTH

When first married, Charles and Catherine lived with her younger sister Mary, who died suddenly aged just 17. Dickens was distraught and this young innocent was subsequently the inspiration for several of Dickens' characters including Little Nell in *The Old Curiosity Shop*.

NELLY TERNAN

Ellen 'Nelly' Ternan was a young actress who Dickens met while performing in *The Frozen Deep*, a play by his friend, the author Wilkie Collins. Dickens left his wife when Catherine discovered a gold bracelet that he had bought for Nelly. It is widely believed that Nelly became his mistress.

KEY mother first love wife friend

 possible mistress tragic inspiration

DICKENS' LATER LIFE

Once he became a full-time writer, Dickens was constantly active, working on several projects at once. He was usually progressing at least one serialized novel, but was generally writing other articles and stories at the same time, editing a magazine, involved in various amateur theatricals, meeting and dining with friends and family, and, later, pursuing a punishing schedule of readings of his work to the public.

1838
Oliver Twist is published. Dickens visits schools in northern England in preparation for his next book.

1844
Dickens and family visit Italy, Switzerland and France.

1846
Becomes editor of the *Daily News* but resigns after 17 issues. *Dombey and Son* is published.

1839
Nicholas Nickleby is published.

1843
A Christmas Carol is published in December, beginning Dickens' tradition of an annual Christmas book.

1847
Helps Angela Burdett-Coutts set up and run a home for fallen women.

1840
Dickens launches a new weekly periodical, *Master Humphrey's Clock*, which runs until December 1841.

1842
Dickens visits the USA for the first time. He publishes *American Notes* on his return. *Martin Chuzzlewit* is published.

1850
Dickens' new weekly magazine *Household Words* begins publication.

1851

Dickens' father dies.

1852

Bleak House is published. Dickens gives his first public readings the following year.

1856

Dickens buys Gad's Hill Place in Rochester, Kent.

1859

Dickens starts a new journal, *All The Year Round* (published weekly).

1858

Dickens separates from his wife Catherine.

1857

Author Hans Christian Andersen visits Gad's Hill. Dickens acts in Wilkie Collins' play T*he Frozen Deep*.

1860

Great Expectations is published.

1867

Dickens takes a second trip to the USA, with readings in Boston, New York, Washington and elsewhere.

1870

The first six-monthly parts of *The Mystery of Edwin Drood* are published.

1863

Dickens' mother and his son Walter both die, Walter while he is in India, serving in the army.

1865

Dickens is involved in the Staplehurst train crash, with Ellen Ternan and her mother, but is not injured.

1870

Dickens dies on 9 June, after collapsing at Gad's Hill. He is buried in Westminster Abbey.

LIFE

A DAY IN THE LIFE OF DICKENS

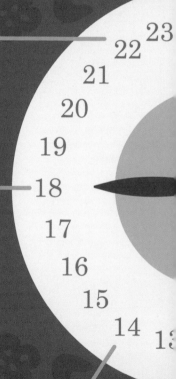

MIDNIGHT

Dickens retired for the night.

10pm

Dickens spent the latter part of the evening with family or friends. He loved company and socialising.

6pm

Dickens dined, often with friends – these meals could go on for several hours, depending on the company.

2pm

Short break for lunch followed by a three-hour walk in the city or countryside. During this time, he mulled over story lines, characters and ideas.

23 22 21 20 19 18 17 16 15 14 13

Dickens was a man with boundless energy, and he drove himself hard to utilize it in a variety of ways. He kept to a strict daily timetable and ensured his surroundings were meticulously tidy. Even when staying away from home, his first task was to tidy the room to make it the perfect workspace.

He was incredibly prolific. He wrote 15 large novels, numerous short stories and essays and was, for much of his working life, editing a magazine as well. In addition, Dickens was involved in many amateur theatrical productions and regularly met with other writers and actors, as well as travelling around the country and abroad.

01
02
03
04
05
06
07
08
09
10
11

7am
Wake up

8am
Breakfast

9am
Working time

Dickens needed quiet and seclusion to work, a fresh vase of flowers on his desk and his quill pens in the usual place. He generally wrote at least 2,000 words a day but even when words didn't come easily, he stuck to his schedule, doodling or thinking at his desk.

10 THINGS YOU MIGHT NOT KNOW ABOUT CHARLES DICKENS

01 BIRD LOVER

Dickens had a pet raven called Grip, which made an appearance in *Barnaby Rudge*. Author Edgar Allan Poe reviewed the book and was fascinated by the raven. Many believe that Grip inspired Poe's 1845 poem *The Raven*.

02 MESMERIST

Dickens became fascinated by mesmerism (hypnosis) and learned the technique. At first he practised it on his wife and children only, but subsequently he helped heal several friends.

03 NO FAIRY-TALE ENDING

Hans Christian Andersen was invited to visit Dickens and family, but seems to have overstayed his welcome. After his departure, Dickens left a card above the dressing-room mirror, which read: "Hans Andersen slept in this room for five weeks – which seemed to the family AGES."

04 DOWN WITH THE KIDS

Dickens was a lover of nicknames, styling himself as 'The Inimitable' and using a variety of pet names for his children. Francis was nicknamed "Chickenstalker", Alfred was "Skittles", Kate was "Lucifer Box" and his 10th child Edward was nicknamed "Plorn".

05
GOOD NIGHT

Dickens would always sleep facing north, rearranging furniture in any room where he slept so that the bed faced north to south. He would then lie in the middle of the mattress, arms extended sideways, in a bid to beat insomnia.

06
CAT'S PAW

When his devoted cat Bob died, Dickens made a letter-opener from his paw. It is now on display in the New York Public Library.

07
NOT ALL IT SEEMS

In his study at Gad's Hill Place, Dickens had a fake bookcase, which was actually a secret door.

08
MAGIC MOMENTS

Dickens was an amateur magician, often entertaining friends and family, with his friend John Forster assisting him. Jane Carlyle (wife of the writer Thomas Carlyle) called him "the best conjuror I ever saw".

09
LITTLE RED RIDING HOOD

In an essay in *Household Words*, Dickens revealed that his first love was Little Red Riding Hood from the children's story.

10
IN THE MONEY

Dickens has appeared on the British £10 note from 1992 until 2000. He was replaced by Charles Darwin and, in 2017, by Jane Austen.

Dickens died of a stroke at Gad's Hill Place in Rochester on 9 June 1870. It was originally planned for him to be buried in Rochester Cathedral, but following a public outcry led by *The Times* newspaper, he was buried in Poet's Corner in Westminster Abbey, London.

In his will he requested "that my name be inscribed in plain English letters on my tomb. I rest my claims to the remembrance of my country upon my published works".

The simple inscription in the Abbey reads:

CHARLES DICKENS, BORN 7th FEBRUARY 1812, DIED 9th JUNE 1870

"IN THE MOONLIGHT WHICH IS ALWAYS SAD, AS THE LIGHT OF THE SUN ITSELF IS — AS THE LIGHT CALLED HUMAN LIFE IS — AT ITS COMING AND ITS GOING."

—Charles Dickens, *A Tale of Two Cities*, 1859

DICKENS' DEATH

FUNERAL

Dickens' funeral was a small and very private ceremony, early in the morning on 14 June. But, after that, so many mourners wanted to visit that the grave was kept open for two days. Flowers were still being left several days later.

....

12 Number of mourners at funeral (just close family and friends).

....

10,000+

Number of mourners who visited the grave to pay their respects in the two days after the funeral.

OTHER WRITERS BURIED AT POET'S CORNER:

Dickens was buried alongside such famous authors as Geoffrey Chaucer, Edmund Spenser, Richard Sheridan and Samuel Johnson. Writers buried there after Dickens include Thomas Hardy; Alfred, Lord Tennyson (right); and Rudyard Kipling.

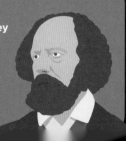

02
WORLD

"IT WAS THE BEST OF TIMES, IT WAS THE WORST OF TIMES."

—Charles Dickens, *A Tale of Two Cities,* 1859

BRITANNIA RULES THE WAVES

RULE BRITANNIA

'Rule, Britannia!' is a British patriotic song, originating from the poem by James Thomson and set to music by Thomas Arne in 1740. The change of lyrics from 'Britannia, rule the waves' to 'Britannia rules the waves' occurred in the Victorian era.

AFRICA

Britain was involved in what became known as the 'Scramble for Africa' as European powers carved up the continent between them. Mrs Jellyby (a philanthropic comic character in *Bleak House*) is more concerned with helping a distant African tribe than her own family.

NORTH AMERICA

After the USA gained independence in 1776, Canada remained a part of the British Empire, along with parts of the Caribbean. Dickens travelled twice to the USA and set parts of *Martin Chuzzlewit* there.

INDIA

The British first went to India in the 17th century to trade through the East India Company. After a rebellion by Indian soldiers in 1857, the Crown took over management of the country and in 1876 Queen Victoria was declared Empress of India. Dickens' son Walter joined the East India Company and then the British Army in India.

 British Empire territories

Dickens lived at a time when Britain was a dominant force across the globe. Britain controlled various areas of the world in its growing Empire (including parts of Africa, India, the Far East, the Caribbean, Canada and Australia) and some of the most important sea routes around the globe, underpinning its strength. Britain adopted the role of global policeman (a period known as the 'Pax Britannica') and controlled the economies of a number of countries, including China. The 19th century is often described as 'Britain's Imperial Century' and the Empire played a significant role in both Dickens' life and his books.

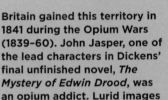

RUSSIA

Britain, France and the Ottoman Empire waged war against Russia during the Crimean War (1853-6) to try to limit Russia's expansionist plans. The invention of the telegraph meant that the public had a more immediate idea of how the war was faring. There was much criticism of administrative incompetence, which inspired Dickens' creation of the Circumlocution Office in *Little Dorrit*.

HONG KONG

Britain gained this territory in 1841 during the Opium Wars (1839-60). John Jasper, one of the lead characters in Dickens' final unfinished novel, *The Mystery of Edwin Drood*, was an opium addict. Lurid images of opium dens were a regular feature of Victorian fiction, the opium users being mainly sailors who had become addicted in the Far East.

AUSTRALIA

Following its establishment as a penal colony in 1788, the British colony in Australia grew in importance throughout the 19th century. The plot of *Great Expectations* revolves around the convict Magwitch who returns to England from Australia.

LONDON LIFE

Dickens lived most of his life in London. During his childhood, the family moved numerous times, mainly due to his father's money problems. As an adult, he knew London inside out, walking its streets for hours, and London subsequently formed the backdrop to most of his novels.

LONDON LANDMARKS IN DICKENS' NOVELS:

Houses of Parliament

London Bridge

St Paul's Cathedral

Tower of London

LANDMARK APPEARANCES IN DICKENS' NOVELS:

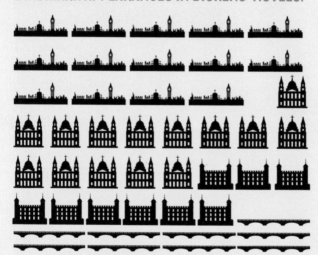

TAVISTOCK HOUSE

Between 1851 and 1858, the large Dickens family needed an even larger house.

10 NORFOLK STREET

Dickens enjoyed his first taste of the city between 1815 and 1817.

16 BAYHAM STREET

Home between 1822 and 1824 was a small terraced house in an area biographer John Forster referred to as "about the poorest part of the London suburbs".

29 JOHNSON STREET

In May 1824, John Dickens was released from prison and the family moved back in together. Three years later, after non-payment of rates, they were evicted.

ISLINGTON

CAMDEN

WESTMINSTER

KENSINGTON & CHELSEA

13 & 16 FURNIVAL'S INN

In 1834, Dickens took a room at number 13. After his marriage to Catherine, the couple returned – to number 16 – in 1836, living in a new furnished suite, with his brother Fred and Catherine's sister Mary.

1 DEVONSHIRE TERRACE

In December 1839, with a growing family, Dickens moved to this elegant house across from Regent's Park.

48 DOUGHTY STREET

Dickens lived here for two years from 1837. This house had 14 rooms on five floors, including basement and attic, with a small garden to the rear. Dickens completed *The Pickwick Papers* here, and wrote *Oliver Twist* and *Nicholas Nickleby*. The house is now the Charles Dickens Museum.

11 SELWOOD TERRACE

Dickens moved here briefly, between 1835 and 1836, to be closer to his fiancée Catherine Hogarth, writing her many affectionate love letters.

VICTORIAN LONDON

During Dickens' lifetime, London's population grew from 1.4 million to 4 million, with many more coming into the city each day to work. In the mid-19th century, London was the busiest city in the world – only by the end of the century would it be rivalled by cities such as Paris and New York. The streets of London were packed day and night with a multitude of street sellers, all shouting out to advertise their wares and to attract customers. It is estimated that by 1850 there were over 30,000 adults (and an unknown number of children) selling on the streets of London.

The 19th century also saw a transformation in the London landscape – major new buildings, squares, streets and transportation all appeared during this time.

KEY DEVELOPMENTS

1829
The Metropolitan Police is established

1855
The Daily Telegraph is first published

1858
The first sewerage system is authorized

1862
Construction begins on the Thames Embankment

1863
The London Underground opens

EUSTON STATION
1837

PADDINGTON STATION
1838

NELSON'S COLUMN
1843

POPULATION

1.4m	1.6m	1.9m	2.2m	2.8m	3.1m	4m
1811	1821	1831	1841	1851	1861	1871

CRYSTAL PALACE
1851

VICTORIA &
ALBERT MUSEUM
1852

BIG BEN
1859

The Great Exhibition

One of the high points of the Victorian age was the Great Exhibition of the Works of Industry of All Nations, held in the magnificent Crystal Palace in Hyde Park, London. It opened in May 1851 and ran for six months. Although the exhibition featured items from countries across the globe, and not just the Empire, its primary aim was to promote Britain as a world leader in industrial development.

TOTAL NUMBER OF VISITORS:

6 million

AVERAGE DAILY ATTENDANCE:

42,831

ONE THIRD OF THE UK POPULATION VISITED

14,000
EXHIBITS

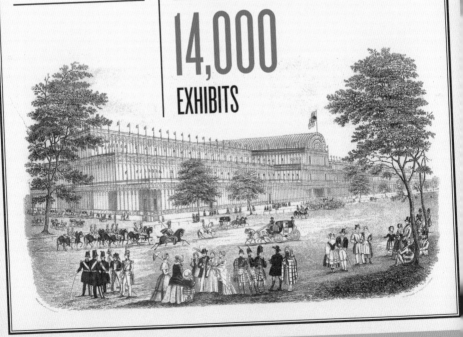

EXHIBITS INCLUDED:

Adding machines, a huge hydraulic press, a Steam hammer printing press that produced 5,000 copies of the *Illustrated London News* every hour, a cigarette-making machine, steam engines, railway locomotives, firearms, early versions of the bicycle and the world's largest diamond – the Koh-i-noor.

THE CRYSTAL PALACE

108 ft (33 m)

1,848 ft (563 m)

Designed by Joseph Paxton, the Great Exhibition building was made of cast iron and plate glass. After the exhibition, the building was rebuilt in Sydenham, South London, in 1854, and the area nearby was renamed Crystal Palace. The Crystal Palace was destroyed by fire in 1936.

DICKENS' VISIT

Although Dickens applauded the fantastic displays of scientific and technological progress at the Exhibition, he wasn't as impressed as many others when he visited in July 1851, describing it as "a very Fortunatus's purse of boredom".

OTHER FAMOUS VISITORS

- Charles Darwin (left)
- Lewis Carroll
- George Eliot
- Alfred, Lord Tennyson
- Charlotte Brontë

GETTING AROUND

WALKING 3mph

By the mid-19th century, over 200,000 people walked into London daily. By 1870, that number was over 750,000.

OMNIBUS

6mph

PASSENGERS:

Up to 26

STAGECOACH

12mph

PASSENGERS:

Approx. 20

When Dickens was born in 1812, the main form of public transportation around London was either walking or, for those who could afford it, riding in a carriage pulled by horses. By the time of his death in 1870, there was a much wider variety of public transport, steam trains were commonplace and journey times were subsequently quicker. London's streets also became even busier – crammed full of pedestrians, horses and all the many different types of transport. These dramatic changes were reflected in Dickens' writings, from the coach and horses in the early novels such as *The Pickwick Papers* and *Nicholas Nickleby,* to the steam train that kills Carker in *Dombey and Son.*

STEAM TRAIN 22mph

PASSENGERS:
By 1845 over 30 million passengers were being carried annually in the UK.

FIRST TRAIN LINE:
London to Birmingham (112 miles), opened in 1838.

HACKNEY CAB 5–10mph

PASSENGERS:
2/3

UNDERGROUND 30–40mph

PASSENGERS:
Carried 38,000 passengers on the first day of the London Underground.

FIRST UNDERGROUND LINE:
This ran from Paddington to Farringdon, opening in 1863.

DETAILS:
Gas-lit wooden carriages, pulled by steam locomotives

EXPANSION:
More lines followed and electric trains were introduced in 1890.

STEAMER 5–10mph

PASSENGERS:
13,000 daily

NUMBER OF BOATS:
Around the mid-19th century, one steamer ran between London Bridge and Westminster Bridge every 4 minutes.

THE STAPLEHURST TRAIN CRASH

After the first commercial train journey, by Robert Stephenson's *Rocket* at the opening of the Liverpool and Manchester Railway in 1830, railways quickly spread across the country and became the fastest mode of transport (up to 80 miles per hour). However, such speeds had consequences. The first casualty was the MP William Huskisson who was run down and killed by the *Rocket* on that first journey. More deaths and injuries followed, including those resulting from the famous Staplehurst train crash in 1865, which involved Charles Dickens himself. Dickens, shaken by the incident, was forever after nervous about travelling by train. He died five years to the day after the accident.

Date:
9 June 1865

Time:
3:13pm

Location:
Staplehurst, Kent

Route:
South Eastern Main Lane

Train:
South Eastern Railway, Folkestone to London

Incident:
Train derailed crossing the 10-foot (3-m)-high Beult Viaduct

2 2nd-CLASS CARRIAGES 3 BRAKE VANS

UNDAMAGED

CAUSE
A length of track had been removed for engineering work, leaving a 42-foot (13-m) gap.

WARNING
A warning flag was waved at 554 yards (0.5 km) from the gap, but the train could not stop in time. Had the warning distance been doubled, the train could have been saved.

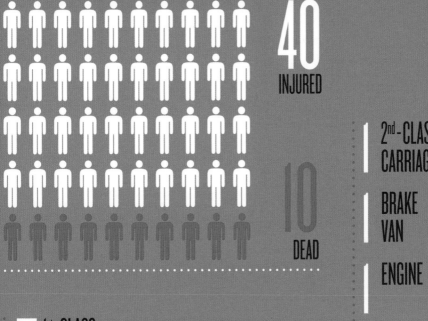

40 INJURED

10 DEAD

2nd-CLASS CARRIAGE

BRAKE VAN

ENGINE

UNDAMAGED

7 1st-CLASS CARRIAGES DESTROYED

DICKENS' INVOLVEMENT IN THE CRASH

- Charles Dickens was in the leading first-class carriage with his mistress Ellen Ternan and her mother (returning from France) – they were uninjured.

- Their first-class carriage did not fall into the river below, but was hanging dangerously from the edge of the viaduct.

- Dickens first rescued Ellen and her mother. He then spent several hours tending to other passengers, giving them brandy and hot water from his hat.

- Later Dickens salvaged the manuscript of *Our Mutual Friend* from his carriage.

- Dickens was recognized, and the next day the incident featured in the *Illustrated London News*.

DICKENS AND THE WORKHOUSE

Having seen and experienced poverty up close as a child, Dickens was always interested in the fate of the poor and the less fortunate. Up to 25 per cent of the population lived in some form of poverty in his lifetime. The 1834 Poor Law Amendment Act tried to deal with this problem by building workhouses. The aim of the workhouse was to discourage people from claiming poor relief, and conditions were made as forbidding as possible. Like many others, Dickens hated the workhouse system and thought that it victimized the poor.

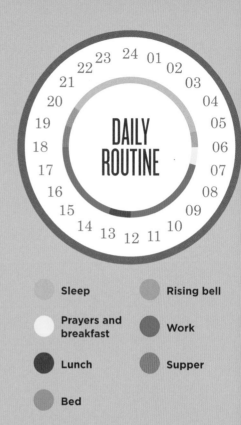

DAILY ROUTINE

23 24 01 02 03 04 05 06 07 08 09 10 11 12 13 14 15 16 17 18 19 20 21 22

- Sleep
- Rising bell
- Prayers and breakfast
- Work
- Lunch
- Supper
- Bed

500
Number of extra workhouses (or 'spikes') built after the act of 1834

FOOD:

BREAKFAST:
Gruel and bread

DINNER:
Boiled meat three days
a week, otherwise soup

SUPPER:
Bread and cheese

On arrival at the workhouse, inmates were split into
one of seven groups and remained separated:

| Women infirm through age or illness | Men infirm through age or illness | Able-bodied women over 15 years old | Able-bodied men over 15 years old |

| Girls aged between 7 and 15 | Boys aged between 7 and 15 | Children under the age of 7 |

7 DIFFERENT GROUPS

OLIVER TWIST

Dickens wrote the novel to highlight the system's
harsh treatment of an innocent child born and
raised in a workhouse. He described the neglect,
ill-treatment and hunger.

TO BE CONTINUED...
THE CRAZE FOR SERIAL NOVELS

The Pickwick Papers
Charles Dickens
Published in 19 parts

19 PARTS

1836–37

The Count of Monte Cristo
Alexandre Dumas
Serialized in the
Journal des Debats

18 PARTS

1844–46

The Woman in White
Wilkie Collins
Serialized in *All the Year Round*

40 PARTS

1859–60

MAGAZINE DAY

New editions of monthly journals were published on the last weekday of each month in Britain and were eagerly awaited. Many writers became adept at writing in instalments, often leaving cliffhangers at the end of an issue, thus building excitement for the next issue. Dickens' *The Old Curiosity Shop* (1840–41) is a great example, as readers were desperate to know the fate of the beloved character Little Nell.

20,000 Leagues Under the Sea
Jules Verne
Serialized in the
Magasin d'Education

16 PARTS

1869–70

It was during the Victorian era that publishing novels in serial form became popular. Prior to that time, serious novelists had wanted to be published in hardback volumes, looking down on serial fiction. The success of Dickens' *The Pickwick Papers* (1836) changed this and demonstrated the viability and success of the format. Serial fiction kept readers coming back to buy further issues and the success of many magazines was built on this trend. This subsequently became the norm in the USA (with magazines such as *Harper's* and *The Atlantic Monthly* growing during this period) and across Europe, too. Publishers then got a second bite of the cherry when they published the complete novel in hardback volumes.

Vanity Fair
William Makepeace Thackeray
Serialized in *Punch*

20 PARTS

1847–48

Uncle Tom's Cabin
Harriet Beecher Stowe
Serialized in the *National Era*

10 PARTS

1851–52

Wives and Daughters
Elizabeth Gaskell
Serialized in *The Cornhill Magazine*

20 PARTS

1864–66

Crime and Punishment
Fyodor Dostoyevsky
Serialized in *Russian Messenger*

12 PARTS

1866

Middlemarch
George Eliot
Published in 8 parts

8 PARTS

1871–72

Far from the Madding Crowd
Thomas Hardy
Serialized in *The Cornhill Magazine*

12 PARTS

1874

Portrait of a Lady
Henry James
Serialized in *The Atlantic Monthly*

12 PARTS

1880–81

ROYAL CONNECTIONS

Dickens was commissioned to write a small book, *Sketches of Young Couples*, to cash in on Victoria's marriage to Prince Albert in 1840.

Queen Victoria, her enlightened age and her Empire were constants throughout Dickens' adult life (she became Queen in 1837). Although they only met late in Dickens' life, the Queen was said to be a fan of his work.

Victoria and Albert attended one of Dickens' amateur theatrical productions of *Not So Bad As We Seem* (by Edward Bulwer-Lytton) in 1851.

Dickens and his theatrical troupe put on a special performance of *The Frozen Deep* for the royal party in July 1857, but Dickens declined the summons to meet the Queen afterwards, because he didn't want to meet her when he was in stage dress and make-up.

Dickens and Victoria finally met in March 1870, just months before his death. For reasons of etiquette, Dickens remained standing throughout the 90-minute audience (despite suffering from a swollen foot).

In the early years of Victoria's reign, Dickens and several friends (including Daniel Maclise and John Forster) pretended to be passionately in love with the Queen and were ecstatic when they found pubs called The Queen's Head and The Queen's Arms.

CHARLES DICKENS

03
WORK

"THERE IS NO CONTEMPORARY ENGLISH WRITER WHOSE WORKS ARE READ SO GENERALLY THROUGH THE WHOLE HOUSE...

...WHO CAN GIVE PLEASURE TO THE SERVANTS AS WELL AS TO THE MISTRESS, TO THE CHILDREN AS WELL AS TO THE MASTER."

—Walter Bagehot, journalist and essayist, 1858

KEY WORK: THE PICKWICK PAPERS

Dickens established himself as a writer with *Sketches by Boz*, his observations on London life. But it was the publication of *The Pickwick Papers* that made Dickens a success and ensured his future as a writer. Published in monthly parts, *The Pickwick Papers* was initially perceived by publishers Chapman & Hall as a series of sketches to accompany humorous sporting prints by illustrator Robert Seymour. However, Dickens persuaded the publishers to let him set the agenda and have Seymour illustrate his ideas in what became a series of loosely-related adventures. He conceived the character of Mr Pickwick and began work on the first number, still using the pen-name 'Boz'.

FULL TITLE

The Posthumous Papers of the Pickwick Club containing a faithful record of the Perambulations, Perils, Travels, Adventures and Sporting Transactions of the Corresponding Members.

Edited by "Boz."

The humorous character of cockney Sam Weller was introduced as Mr Pickwick's valet in issue 4. His popularity affected the future direction of the series and contributed to its increased success.

MARCH 1836

Date of first issue. New editions of monthly journals were published on the last weekday of each month.

Illustrator Robert Seymour committed suicide after the second issue. His replacement, 19-year-old 'Phiz' (real name Hablot Knight Browne), took over on issue 4 and became Dickens' illustrator for the next 24 years.

19

The number of monthly editions (the final number in October 1837 was a double issue). There was no issue in May 1837, as Dickens was mourning the death of his sister-in-law Mary Hogarth. It was the only time in his career that he ever missed a deadline.

32

Number of pages per issue. Dickens persuaded his publishers to increase the number from the third issue (previously 26 pages). Later issues included an increasing number of pages of advertisements, too, as the publication's popularity grew.

PRINT FIGURES

First issue

Second issue print run after poor sales

Regular sales figures, once it took off

Sales at its peak

40,000

20,000

500

1,000

THEMES

- **INJUSTICE IN THE JUSTICE SYSTEM**
- **POVERTY**
- **FATHERHOOD**
- **INCARCERATION**
- **MONEY**

THE GRIM REAPER

The average life expectancy in 1840 was just 42, and one in six children died before they were one year old. Charles Dickens' family was no different – he was the second of eight children, but the third (Alfred) died at the age of six months. Dickens and his wife Catherine also lost their daughter Dora at just eight months old and he was heartbroken when his sister-in-law Mary Hogarth died suddenly at the age of 17. Not surprisingly, death features heavily in Dickens' novels.

NUMBER OF MAIN CHARACTERS KILLED OFF IN EACH NOVEL:

BLEAK HOUSE	7
DAVID COPPERFIELD	7
OUR MUTUAL FRIEND	5
GREAT EXPECTATIONS	4
LITTLE DORRIT	4
DOMBEY AND SON	4
NICHOLAS NICKLEBY	4
A TALE OF TWO CITIES	3
BARNABY RUDGE	3
THE OLD CURIOSITY SHOP	3
OLIVER TWIST	3
HARD TIMES	2
MARTIN CHUZZLEWIT	2
THE MYSTERY OF EDWIN DROOD	1
THE PICKWICK PAPERS	1

53

TOTAL NUMBER OF MAIN CHARACTER DEATHS IN DICKENS' NOVELS

MOST GRUESOME DEATHS:

NANCY
(*Oliver Twist*)
Beaten to death

KROOK
(*Bleak House*)
Spontaneous combustion

CARKER
(*Dombey and Son*)
Hit by a train

MISS HAVISHAM
(*Great Expectations*)
In a fire

MOST TEAR-JERKING DEATHS:

LITTLE NELL

(*The Old Curiosity Shop*)
The much loved Little Nell's gradual weakening and death after a tortuous journey created a massive outpouring of grief from readers.

SMIKE

(*Nicholas Nickleby*)
Smike is an orphan living a desperate life in the care of the cruel Wackford Squeers. He dies of tuberculosis.

PAUL DOMBEY

(*Dombey and Son*)
The eponymous elder Paul Dombey is obsessed by money. He puts all his future hopes onto his young son Paul. However, young Paul is a sickly child and dies aged just six years old.

THE DEATH OF LITTLE NELL

Seemingly the whole world was in tears at the death of Little Nell in the serialization of *The Old Curiosity Shop*. New York readers stormed the pier when the ship bearing the final instalment arrived in 1841, desperate to know the outcome. Reading this finale on a train, Irish leader Daniel O'Connell famously burst into tears and threw the book out of the window. However, Dickens' highly sentimental narrative didn't appeal to everyone – Oscar Wilde wrote: "One would have to have a heart of stone to read the death of little Nell without dissolving into tears... of laughter."

WORK

MEMORABLE CHARACTERS

SAM WELLER

CHARACTER:
Cheeky cockney manservant.

STORY:
Becomes companion to
Mr Pickwick on his travels.

END:
Continues in Mr Pickwick's household
when latter retires from his travels.

FACT:
Sam's cockney mode of speech and
his way of quoting people led to the
term 'Wellerism'.

CATCHPHRASE:
"Out vith it, as the father said to his
child, when he swallowed a farden."

OLIVER TWIST

CHARACTER:
Orphan, born in workhouse.

STORY:
Falls in with a gang of thieves.

END:
Saved by a benefactor who discovers
Oliver's true background and adopts
him.

FACT:
The most famous adaptation of this
book is Lionel Bart's musical *Oliver!*,
which includes the song 'Food,
Glorious Food'.

CATCHPHRASE:
"Please, sir, I want some more."

FAGIN

CHARACTER:
Street thief and miser, leader of a
gang of criminal children.

STORY:
Beats the children and teaches
Oliver how to steal.

END:
Captured and sentenced to hang.

FACT:
Dickens worked with a boy called
Fagin in the boot-blacking factory.

CATCHPHRASE:
"My dear."

URIAH HEEP

CHARACTER:
Lawyer, famed for cloying humility
and sycophancy.

STORY:
Evil antagonist throughout David
Copperfield's life.

END:
Jailed.

FACT:
There is a British rock band called
Uriah Heep.

CATCHPHRASE:
"I am far too 'umble."

MR MICAWBER

CHARACTER:
Clerk, constantly living beyond his means and always in debt.

STORY:
Befriends David Copperfield.

END:
Emigrates to Australia, becomes a banker and a magistrate.

FACT:
Mr Micawber is an eternal optimist, supported by his loyal and long-suffering wife, Emma.

CATCHPHRASE:
"Something will turn up."

A great deal of Dickens' success was due to the popularity of his many remarkable characters. With his novels being published in monthly instalments, readers had time to get to know the characters and anticipate their next appearance. Dickens was a brilliant observer of human life and used this skill to create his memorable, much-loved characters. Many of them remain part of our cultural landscape today.

KEY TO BOOKS

The Pickwick Papers

A Christmas Carol

Oliver Twist

David Copperfield

Great Expectations

EBENEZER SCROOGE

CHARACTER:
Cold-hearted moneylender and miser who hates Christmas.

STORY:
Meets three ghosts who make him see his faults.

END:
Turns over a new leaf, becomes nice to people – and loves Christmas!

FACT:
There were many supposed real-life models for Scrooge, including John Elwes (1714–89), a noted British eccentric and miser.

CATCHPHRASE:
"Bah! Humbug!"

MISS HAVISHAM

CHARACTER:
Jilted on her wedding day, still wears her wedding dress and has a rotting wedding cake on her table.

STORY:
Trains her adopted daughter Estella to break the hearts of men.

END:
Repents before dying from injuries sustained in a fire.

FACT:
Said to be based on a real person (Eliza Donnithorne) who was jilted on her wedding day.

CATCHPHRASE:
"Break their hearts!"

DAVID COPPERFIELD

David Copperfield is Dickens' eighth novel, published in book form in 1850, illustrated by Phiz. *David Copperfield* is a thinly-disguised autobiography and was Dickens' first book written in the first person. Dickens seemed to treasure it above all his novels. It was only after his death and the publication of John Forster's biography that the reading public realized how autobiographical *David Copperfield* really was, learning for the first time about Dickens' tough childhood.

FULL TITLE:

The Personal History, Adventures, Experience and Observation of David Copperfield the Younger of Blunderstone Rookery (Which He never meant to be Published on any Account).

1849–50

Publication of serialized instalments by Bradbury & Evans. It was published in book form in 1850.

19

Number of monthly instalments

PLOT:

After his mother's death, David is sent to work in a bottling factory by his stepfather, Mr Murdstone, but runs away to live with his aunt Betsey Trotwood. His friends Steerforth and Tommy Traddles reappear throughout the narrative, to help David on his adventures. The story concludes with Copperfield, like Dickens himself, eventually becoming a successful author.

REAL-LIFE CHARACTERS:

DORA
David's first wife – based on Dickens' first love Maria Beadnell (even including her dog Jip)

AGNES
David's second wife – based on a combination of Mary and Georgina Hogarth

MR MICAWBER –
based on Dickens' father, John Dickens

DAVID'S NAMES:

David is rarely called 'David' in the novel but appears under a variety of other names:

DAVY · TROT · COPPERFIELD · TROTWOOD · DAISY · DOADY

THEMES

- CHILD EXPLOITATION
- EQUALITY IN MARRIAGE
- CLASS
- WEALTH

CHAPTER 55 TEMPEST

This is one of the most memorable passages in Dickens' entire work, where most of the key plot lines of the book come to a dramatic and tragic conclusion during a raging storm in the sea at Yarmouth. Dickens drew on all his imaginary powers in this climactic chapter – his friend John Forster said it was: "A description that may compare with the most impressive in the language."

DICKENS ON TOUR

In 1853 Dickens gave his first public reading of his work, as a one-off event for charity. However, it was such a success that readings soon became a more regular activity and continued almost to his death. Dickens was a great performer and the audience hung on his every word as he played all the characters. He adapted the narrative to make the readings as effective as possible, writing stage directions to himself in the margins of his notes.

After his return from his second visit to the USA, and in failing health, Dickens began a farewell tour of Britain in October 1868, including a dramatic reading of the murder of Nancy from *Oliver Twist*. The energy and passion involved in this performance seems to have taken its toll and may well have contributed to Dickens' early death the following year.

1858 – 59 BRITISH TOUR

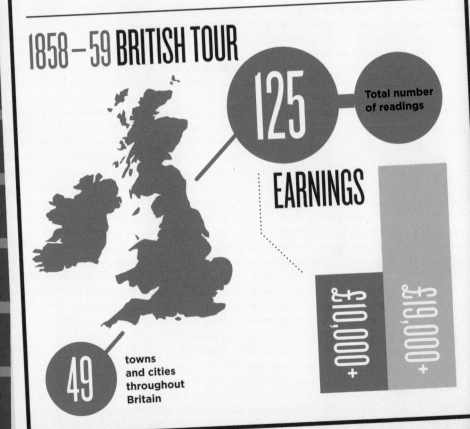

125 Total number of readings

49 towns and cities throughout Britain

EARNINGS

£10,000 +

£19,000 +

1867–68 USA TOUR

Cities visited included New York, Boston, Philadelphia, Washington, Syracuse and Baltimore.

75 | 5
readings | months

ESSENTIAL PROPS:

Specially made reading desk

Gas lighting

Manuscript with stage directions

Maroon backdrop

MOST POPULAR STORIES PERFORMED:

| A Christmas Carol | Oliver Twist | The Chimes | The Cricket on the Hearth | The Pickwick Papers |

DICKENS IN THE USA

START

It is 1842. You are Charles Dickens, writer of bestsellers such as *The Pickwick Papers* and *Oliver Twist*, and you have just arrived in Boston with your wife Catherine to a hero's welcome.

Cheering crowd greet you everywhere you go.
GO FORWARD TWO SPACES.

A 'Boz Ball' is he in your honour a the Park Theater NY, attended by 3,000 people.
GO FORWARD TWO SPACES.

You are disappointed by conditions in the slums and prisons.
GO BACK TWO SPACES.

Returning to North America, you are impressed by Niagara Falls and enjoy Canada.
GO FORWARD THREE SPACES.

You send your title character in *Martin Chuzzlewit* to the USA, using the book to disparage the US press.
GO BACK TO START.

MARTIN CHUZZLEWIT

CHARLES DICKENS

DICKENS

You travel to New York. **GO FORWARD ONE SPACE.**

You make a speech about international copyright. The press are furious. GO BACK ONE SPACE.

ou see slavery rst-hand in chmond, rginia. D BACK NE SPACE.

You take the riverboat to St Louis, but call the Mississippi "that miserable river". MISS A GO.

You return home to England and write *American Notes,* criticizing the US way of life. GO BACK THREE SPACES.

ou include a note in future ditions of *American* otes and *Martin uzzlewit* praising the mense improvements the country. O TO FINISH.

FINISH

WORK

KEY WORK:
GREAT EXPECTATIONS

Great Expectations remains one of Dickens' best-loved novels. Like *David Copperfield*, it is written in the first person and follows the development of the central character from boyhood to adulthood. It is not, however, autobiographical to the same extent.

IN THE END?

ORIGINAL ENDING:
Pip sees Estella remarry after becoming Bentley Drummle's widow (thought to be too sad an ending by friends who read the text before publication).

ENDING CHANGED TO:
Pip meets Estella and they go off together – "I saw no shadow of another parting from her."

36
Weekly parts, serialized in Dickens' *All The Year Round* magazine between December 1860 and August 1861. Published in volume form later that year.

100,000
Copies of the serialization sold each week (midway through its run)

BILDUNGSROMAN

Great Expectations is regarded as a great example of a *bildungsroman* – a story depicting the personal growth and development of a character – in this case, the orphan Pip. All the other characters revolve around his central story and become entwined in his development.

01 **JOE GARGERY**
Pip's brother-in-law and a blacksmith

02 **MRS JOE GARGERY**
Pip's older sister

03 **BIDDY**
Friend of Pip and potential partner

04 **ABEL MAGWITCH**
Escaped convict, who Pip helps, and who then becomes Pip's benefactor

05 **MISS HAVISHAM**
Wealthy spinster, who engages Pip as a companion for her adopted daughter Estella

06 **ESTELLA**
Brought up to break men's hearts, Pip's love interest

07 **JAGGERS**
London lawyer who represents both Magwitch and Miss Havisham

08 **JOHN WEMMICK**
Clerk to Mr Jaggers and friend to Pip

09 **COMPEYSON**
Convict, enemy of Magwitch, originally engaged to marry Miss Havisham in an effort to steal her fortune

10 **ORLICK**
Apprentice blacksmith at Joe's forge and enemy of Pip

11 **BENTLEY DRUMMLE**
Coarse young man who is Pip's rival for the love of Estella.

"I LOVED HER AGAINST REASON, AGAINST PROMISE, AGAINST PEACE, AGAINST HOPE, AGAINST HAPPINESS, AGAINST ALL DISCOURAGEMENT THAT COULD BE."

—Pip, of his love for Estella, *Great Expectations*, 1850

THEMES

- CLASS/WEALTH
- SELF IMPROVEMENT
- AMBITION
- CRIME/GUILT
- CONSCIENCE
- THE CITY/LONDON
- IMPERIALISM

MAGAZINE EDITOR

As a young writer, Dickens contributed to newspapers and magazines with observational articles, mainly about London life. He edited magazines throughout his working life, believing that they underpinned his close relationship with his readers. As well as editing submissions from other writers, he contributed articles and stories. This was a huge commitment of time, in addition to his writing 15 major novels.

BENTLEY'S MISCELLANY

DURATION:	1837–68
FREQUENCY:	Monthly
EDITOR:	Dickens (until 1839), William Harrison Ainsworth (to 1868)
SERIALIZATIONS:	*Oliver Twist*
CONTRIBUTORS:	Wilkie Collins, Thomas Love Peacock, Edgar Allan Poe

BENTLEY'S

MISCELLANY.

VOL I.

LONDON:
RICHARD BENTLEY,
NEW BURLINGTON STREET.
1837

MASTER HUMPHREY'S CLOCK

DURATION:	1840–1
FREQUENCY:	Weekly
EDITOR:	Dickens
SERIALIZATIONS:	*The Old Curiosity Shop* and *Barnaby Rudge*
CONTRIBUTORS:	Dickens wrote the whole magazine

PEAK SALES (IN THOUSANDS):

0	50	100

DAILY NEWS

Dickens founded the new daily newspaper in 1846 and edited the first 17 issues as well.

HOUSEHOLD WORDS

"Familiar in their Mouths as HOUSEHOLD WORDS."—SHAKESPEARE.

HOUSEHOLD WORDS.
A WEEKLY JOURNAL.
CONDUCTED BY CHARLES DICKENS.

DURATION:	1850–9
FREQUENCY:	Weekly
EDITOR:	Dickens
SERIALIZATIONS:	*Hard Times*
CONTRIBUTORS:	Wilkie Collins, Elizabeth Gaskell

ALL THE YEAR ROUND

"THE STORY OUR LIVES FROM YEAR TO YEAR."—SHAKESPEARE.

ALL THE YEAR ROUND.
A WEEKLY JOURNAL.
CONDUCTED BY CHARLES DICKENS.

A TALE OF TWO CITIES.

DURATION:	1859–95
FREQUENCY:	Weekly
EDITOR:	Dickens (his son Charley took over after Dickens' death in 1870)
SERIALIZATIONS:	*A Tale of Two Cities* and *Great Expectations*
CONTRIBUTORS:	Wilkie Collins, Elizabeth Gaskell, Edward Bulwer-Lytton

CHARLES DICKENS

15 novels, numerous short stories, essays and non-fiction. His final novel, *The Mystery of Edwin Drood,* was unfinished at his death.

Married Catherine Hogarth and had 10 children

58

BORN: 1812 DIED: 1870

4 magazines edited: *Bentley's Miscellany, Master Humphrey's Clock, Household Words* and *All The Year Round.*

His autobiographical novel *David Copperfield* was serialized 1849–50.

WILLIAM MAKEPEACE THACKERAY

13 novels, numerous short stories, essays and non-fiction. His final novel, *Denis Duval,* was unfinished at his death.

His autobiographical novel *The History of Pendennis* was serialized 1848–50.

Married Isabella Gethin Shawe and had three children

52

BORN: 1811 DIED: 1863

magazine edited: *The Cornhill Magazine.*

Dickens and Thackeray were close contemporaries, born within a year of each other, and lived parallel lives. They both started their careers as journalists, writing numerous essays and stories before progressing to novels, although Thackeray's success came later than Dickens'. They both published novels in serial form and both subsequently edited magazines, too. They were friends and moved in the same social circles, but fell out in later life. Dickens was always the more successful and has the greater legacy today.

WORK

PHIZ

Books published in serial form in the 19th century were generally accompanied by illustrations. Dickens' illustrators included Robert Seymour, Luke Fildes and George Cruikshank, but the longest-serving was Hablot Knight Browne (1815–82). Browne was apprenticed to an engraver before becoming an illustrator and working for the satirical magazine *Punch*. Phiz first worked with Dickens on *The Pickwick Papers*, after the original illustrator Robert Seymour committed suicide. Phiz's visualizations of key Dickens characters, such as Sam Weller, Mr Micawber, Wackford Squeers, Mrs Gamp and Tom Pinch, helped to cement their popularity with the public.

Browne's pen name was chosen to work with Dickens' 'Boz'. It is believed to be a shortening of 'physiognomy'.

40

Number of his illustrations that can be seen at the Royal Academy in London.

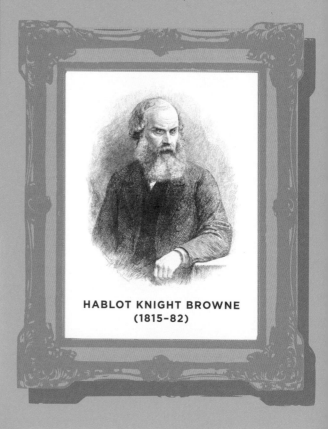

HABLOT KNIGHT BROWNE (1815–82)

In 2012, four Phiz illustrations were issued as stamps by the Royal Mail to mark the 200th anniversary of Dickens' birth.

10

Number of Dickens' books Phiz illustrated:
The Pickwick Papers, Nicholas Nickleby, The Old Curiosity Shop, Barnaby Rudge, Martin Chuzzlewit, Dombey and Son, David Copperfield, Bleak House, Little Dorrit, A Tale of Two Cities.

CHARLES DICKENS

04
LEGACY

"DICKENS ATTACKED ENGLISH INSTITUTIONS WITH A FEROCITY THAT HAS NEVER SINCE BEEN APPROACHED. YET HE MANAGED TO DO IT WITHOUT MAKING HIMSELF HATED, AND, MORE THAN

THIS, THE VERY PEOPLE HE ATTACKED HAVE SWALLOWED HIM SO COMPLETELY THAT HE HAS BECOME A NATIONAL INSTITUTION HIMSELF."

—George Orwell,
Charles Dickens, 1940

WRITING BY NUMBERS

Unlike many of his contemporaries in the 19th-century literary boom, all of Charles Dickens' major works and much of his extensive output of short stories and essays remain in print today. More than 200 years after his birth, his books are still read and loved around the world. His stories and his characters live on and show no signs of declining in support.

THE PICKWICK PAPERS 1836	**OLIVER TWIST** 1837	**NICHOLAS NICKLEBY** 1838	**THE OLD CURIOSITY SHOP** 1840
BARNABY RUDGE 1841	**MARTIN CHUZZLEWIT** 1842	**DOMBEY AND SON** 1846	**DAVID COPPERFIELD** 1849
BLEAK HOUSE 1852	**HARD TIMES** 1854	**LITTLE DORRIT** 1855	**A TALE OF TWO CITIES** 1859
GREAT EXPECTATIONS 1860	**OUR MUTUAL FRIEND** 1864	**THE MYSTERY OF EDWIN DROOD** 1870	**15 NOVELS**

5 CHRISTMAS BOOKS

4 NON-FICTION BOOKS

50+ ESSAYS
20+ SHORT STORIES

A CHRISTMAS CAROL

1843

THE CHIMES

1844

SKETCHES BY BOZ (ESSAYS)

1836

AMERICAN NOTES (TRAVEL)

1842

THE CRICKET ON THE HEARTH

1845

THE BATTLE OF LIFE

1846

PICTURES FROM ITALY (TRAVEL)

1846

A CHILD'S HISTORY OF ENGLAND (FOR CHILDREN)

1851

THE HAUNTED MAN

1848

According to Nielsen Book Data, Dickens was still the **78th** bestselling author in the UK in the first decade of the 21st century.

TIMELINE OF WORKS

1835 1840 1845 1850 1855 1860 1865 1870

ADAPTABILITY

DAVID COPPERFIELD, 1913

There were about 100 films based on Dickens' work made during the silent era, beginning with the six-minute *Scrooge* in 1901. British film director Thomas Bentley's *David Copperfield* was, however, the first feature-length Dickens adaptation.

DAVID COPPERFIELD, 1935

MGM's classic production, directed by George Cukor and adapted by novelist Hugh Walpole, with W. C. Fields outstanding in the role of Mr Micawber.

SCROOGE, 1951

Starring Alastair Sim as Ebenezer Scrooge, and considered to be the definitive adaptation of *A Christmas Carol*, Dickens' much-loved Christmas story.

A TALE OF TWO CITIES, 1958

British adaptation of Dickens' novel of the French Revolution starring Dirk Bogarde.

Dickens' novels are ripe for adaptation in other forms, as they are full to the brim with multiple plots and vivid, colourful characters. During his own time, Dickens' books were often adapted for the stage. More recently there have been many TV and cinematic adaptations of his novels. These film versions range from the silent era, through the early days of black-and-white cinema to the present day, and including musicals and cartoon adaptations.

REAT EXPECTATIONS, 1946

e first of two Dickens adaptations
m British director David Lean. John
ls starred as Pip with Martita Hunt
morable as Miss Havisham. It is
nerally considered to be the best
aptation of this book and possibly the
st Dickens adaptation ever. One of the
st acclaimed British films of all time.

OLIVER TWIST, 1948

David Lean's second Dickens adaptation,
with memorable performances from Alec
Guinness as Fagin and Anthony Newley
as the Artful Dodger. It was originally
banned in the USA, as the anti-semitic
portrayal of Fagin would have raised
strong criticism.

OLIVER!, 1968

Lionel Bart's musical
adaptation, directed
by Carol Reed,
which won six
Oscars, including
Best Picture.

THE MUPPET CHRISTMAS CAROL, 1992

A much-loved adaptation
of the Christmas classic,
with Michael Caine as
Scrooge but all other
roles played by
Muppets, including
Kermit the Frog
as Bob Cratchit.

Creating Christmas

At the start of the 19th century in England, there was a general harking back to the traditions of the 'Old Christmas'. Dickens cannot be said to have invented the modern Christmas, but he played into this nostalgic appetite and, alongside other developments at the time, helped create Christmas celebrations as we know them today. From *A Christmas Carol* onwards, Dickens produced a Christmas book, a Christmas story or a Christmas edition of his magazine *Household Words* every year. Christmas also features in several of his other books, including the festive celebrations in *The Pickwick Papers*.

After completing his fifth Christmas book, Dickens struggled to find the time to continue producing the annual Christmas stories. As a solution, he used his role as editor of *Household Words* to launch a Christmas-themed issue. For each Christmas edition of *Household Words*, Dickens would provide the framework for a story and have other prominent writers, including Elizabeth Gaskell and Wilkie Collins, do the rest.

DICKENS' CHRISTMAS STORIES

A CHRISTMAS DINNER
1835

A CHRISTMAS CAROL
1843

THE CHRISTMAS GOBLINS
1843

THE CHIMES
1844

THE CRICKET ON THE HEARTH
1845

THE BATTLE OF LIFE
1846

THE HAUNTED MAN
1848

A CHRISTMAS TREE
1850

WHAT CHRISTMAS IS, AS WE GROW OLDER
1851

E POOR ATION'S TORY
1852

THE CHILD'S STORY
1852

NOBODY'S STORY
1853

THE SEVEN POOR TRAVELLERS
1854

THE HOLLY-TREE
1855

TYPOGRAPHIC DICKENS

RULE BRITANNIA
A TALE OF TWO CITIES
PORTSMOUTH
PICKWICK
FORSTER
CARLYLE
LINCOLN'S INN

DICKENSIAN
DROOD

NOVELIST
CHARLES

VICTORIA
WELLER
MAGWITCH
CURIOSITY
GAD'S HILL
CRATCHIT
BRITISH EMPIRE
MARLEY
WHIZ-BANG
NEWGATE
FLUMMOX
HUMBUG
MARSHALSEA
SAWBONES
GHOST
GRIP
POOR
ESTELLA

OLIVER TWIST INDUSTRIAL REVOLUTION BOB COLLINS PHIZ WRITER

MICAWBER CHARING CROSS COPPERFIELD AMERICA

THAMES GASKELL FURNIVALS TAVISTOCK

HOGARTH GORM LUMMY

DEVONSHIRE HAVISHAM DORRIT TERNAN DOUGHTY

DICKENS LONDON

DEVIL-MAY-CARE BLEAK SCROOGE DOTHEBOYS

LOMBARD CHRISTMAS STEERFORTH WACKFORD RUDGE

URIAH HEEP WESTMINSTER DOMBEY NORTH HIRON

NICKLEBY SERIAL NOVELS THACKERAY

GONOPH GREAT EXPECTATIONS EDITOR

THE CHARLES DICKENS MUSEUM

Charles Dickens and his family lived at 48 Doughty Street in London for nearly three years from 1837. When the house was put up for sale in 1922, the Dickens Fellowship launched a national appeal to buy it. The Dickens Fellowship, founded in 1902, is a worldwide association of people who share an interest in the life and works of Charles Dickens. It publishes *The Dickensian* magazine three times a year.

48 DOUGHTY STREET

The museum occupies numbers 48 and 49 Doughty Street – visitors enter through number 49 where the gift shop, café and offices are also housed.

MASTER BEDROOM/ DICKENS' DRESSING ROOM

NURSERY

DRAWING ROOM (DICKENS' STUDY BEHIND)

14 ROOMS

DINING ROOM

OPENED:
9 JUNE 1925

5
FLOORS INCLUDING THE BASEMENT AND ATTIC

100,000

Number of items relating to Dickens' life and work housed in the museum (not just from his years at Doughty Street), including furniture, personal effects, paintings, prints, photographs, letters, manuscripts and rare editions.

WRITTEN HERE:

- *The Pickwick Papers*
- *Oliver Twist*
- *Nicholas Nickleby*

LEGACY

SPEAK LIKE DICKENS

Dickens wrote over 4 million words during his career. He introduced a huge number of character names into the English language such as Cratchit, Fezziwig, Micawber, Havisham, Pickwick and Squeers. But he also introduced more than 250 new words – or, at the very least, popularized the use of them. Here are some words or expressions still in regular use today that Dickens gave to the public:

DEVIL-MAY-CARE

"He was a mighty free and easy, roving, devil-may-care sort of person."
(The Pickwick Papers)

SCROOGE

"He was a tight-fisted hand at the grindstone, Scrooge! A squeezing, wrenching, grasping, scraping, clutching, covetous old sinner!"
(A Christmas Carol)

FLUMMOX

"He'll be what the Italians call reg'larly flummoxed."
(The Pickwick Papers)

CONNUBIALITIES

"Stopping some slight connubialities which had begun to pass between Mr. and Mrs. Browdie."
(Nicholas Nickleby)

ON THE RAMPAGE

"My sister 'went on the Rampage,' in a more alarming degree than at any previous period."
(Great Expectations)

BUTTER-FINGERS

"At every bad attempt at a catch, and every failure to stop the ball, he launched his personal displeasure at the head of the devoted individual in such denunciations as 'Ah, ah! – stupid' – 'Now, butter-fingers'."
(The Pickwick Papers)

SAWBONES

"I thought everybody know'd as a sawbones was a surgeon."
(The Pickwick Papers)

HUMBUG

"Bah! Humbug!"
(A Christmas Carol)

RED TAPE

"Britannia is ... like a trussed fowl: skewered through and through with office-pens, and bound hand and foot with red tape."
(David Copperfield)

'THE CREEPS'

"A visitation in her back which she called 'the creeps'."
(David Copperfield)

When the first monthly instalment of *The Mystery of Edwin Drood* was published in April 1870, it was seen as a return to form for Dickens. His last major novel, *Our Mutual Friend*, had been published in 1864. In the intervening years, Dickens had been busy with his public readings and a second visit to the USA. The book was intended to be published in 12 monthly parts. Dickens wrote six parts before his death in June 1870 – three were published while he was alive, the remaining three in the months following his death. There has been continued speculation about how this unfinished novel would have ended, if Dickens had lived to finish it.

OTHER GREAT UNFINISHED NOVELS

SANDITON JANE AUSTEN 1817

BOUVARD ET PECUCHET GUSTAVE FLAUBERT 1880

BILLY BUDD HERMAN MELVILLE 1891

THE CASTLE FRANZ KAFKA 1924

THE LAST TYCOON F SCOTT FITZGERALD 1940

PLOT

The story is set in 'Cloisterham' (based on Rochester in Kent). In an arranged marriage, Edwin Drood is set to marry orphan Rosa when they come of age. However, the two agree to break off the engagement when they realize that they are more friends than lovers. Soon after, Edwin disappears on Christmas Eve, and is presumed dead. There are hints that his murderer may be his uncle John Jasper, who is in love with Rosa.

POSSIBLE ENDINGS?

1

John Jasper killed Edwin Drood and hid his body in the crypt of the church.

(Thomas Power James wrote this ending claiming it came from Dickens from beyond the grave.)

2

Edwin Drood is still alive.

(In 1872, US author Henry Morford wrote an ending in which Edwin Drood survives.)

3

Edwin Drood has been killed by his rival Neville Landless. Neville is the twin brother of Rosa Landless, who befriends Rosa, adding to the multiple plot strands.

There is fairly convincing evidence that Dickens had intended John Jasper to be revealed as the murderer later in the book – his friend and biographer John Forster confirmed this, as did the illustrator Luke Fildes and Dickens' son Charley.

BIOGRAPHIES

Catherine Hogarth Dickens (1815–79)

Born in Edinburgh to newspaper editor George Hogarth. Catherine married Dickens and bore him 10 children before their separation in 1858. She remained loyal to him and on her death she bequeathed her letters from Dickens to the British Museum.

Charles Culliford Boz Dickens (1837–96)

Dickens' first child. A failed business man, he took over editorship of *All the Year Round* magazine after Dickens' death. Charley subsequently wrote the reference books, *Dickens's Dictionary of London* and *Dickens's Dictionary of the Thames*.

Wilkie Collins (1824–89)

Novelist and playwright, most famous for *The Woman in White* and *The Moonstone*. Collins kept separate households with two different women at the same time. He was a great friend of Dickens and wrote for his magazines. They also worked on theatricals together.

William Charles Macready (1793–1873)

Macready was an actor, making his first appearance on the London stage in 1816 and rose to fame thereafter. He was married twice and was godfather to Dickens' daughter Kate. Dickens, in turn, was godfather to Macready's son Henry.

Edward Chapman (1804–80) & William Hall (1800–47)

Dickens' publisher from 1840–4 and again from 1859 until his death. Chapman & Hall also published works by Thackeray, Anthony Trollope, Elizabeth Barrett-Browning and Evelyn Waugh.

Kate Macready Dickens (1839–1929)

When Dickens and Catherine separated, Kate was the only child to stand up to Dickens and side with Catherine. Her second husband was the artist Charles Edward Perugini. She also became a painter and exhibited at the Royal Academy from 1877.

Henry Fielding Dickens (1849–1933)

The eighth of Dickens' 10 children, Henry was nicknamed Harry and had a successful career in the law. He was knighted in 1922 and was the grandfather of author Monica Dickens.

William Makepeace Thackeray (1811–63)

Born in Calcutta, he was a British novelist and poet. His most famous works are *The History of Pendennis*, *Barry Lyndon* and *Vanity Fair*. He also edited *The Cornhill Magazine*. In his lifetime, he was second only to Dickens in terms of success.

Edward Bulwer Lytton Dickens (1852–1902)

Dickens' 10th child (named after the author Edward Bulwer-Lytton), nicknamed Plorn. He emigrated to Australia at the age of 16 and became a Member of Parliament in New South Wales. He died penniless at the age of 49.

Ellen Ternan (1839–1914)

Often known as Nelly, she was an actress best known as Dickens' mistress, for whom he left his wife in 1858. Six years after Dickens' death, Ellen married George Robinson, who never knew about her connection to Dickens. They had two children and ran a boys' school in Margate.

William Bradbury (1799–1869) & Frederick Evans (1804–70)

Printers who became publishers when they bought *Punch* magazine and published Thackeray's *Vanity Fair*. They became Dickens' publisher in 1844, publishing several of his novels and his *Household Words* magazine.

John Forster (1812–76)

Forster was a literary and drama critic, writer and editor. He was a distinguished figure in London literary circles. He published works on Oliver Goldsmith and Shakespeare, before writing the first biography of Dickens in 1874.

family   friend

writer   publisher

INDEX